Classifying Living Things

Mammals

Andrew Solway

Chicago, Illinois

www.heinemannraintree.com
Visit our website to find out more information about Heinemann-Raintree books.

To order:
☎ Phone 888-454-2279
💻 Visit www.heinemannraintree.com to browse our catalog and order online.

© 2003, 2009 Heinemann Library
an imprint of Capstone Global Library, LLC
Chicago, Illinois

Customer Service: 888-454-2279

Visit our website at www.heinemannraintree.com

Edited by Catherine Clarke and Claire Throp
Designed by Victoria Bevan and AMR Design, Ltd.
Original illustrations © Capstone Global Library, LLC.
Illustrations by David Woodroffe
Picture research by Hannah Taylor

Printed and bound in China by Leo Paper Group

13 12 11 10 09
10 9 8 7 6 5 4 3 2 1

Library of Congress Cataloging-in-Publication Data
Solway, Andrew.
    Classifying mammals / Andrew Solway.
        p. cm. -- (Classifying living things)
Summary: Explains what mammals are and how they differ from other animals, with an overview of the life cycle of a variety of mammals, including pouched mammals, seas mammals, flying mammals, and humans.
Includes bibliographical references (p.   ) and index.
    ISBN 978-1-4329-2356-3 (lib. bdg. : hardcover) -- ISBN 978-1-4329-2366-2 (pbk.)
    1. Mammals--Classification--Juvenile literature. 2. Mammals--Juvenile literature. [1. Mammals.] I. Title. II Series.
    QL708 .S66 2003
    599--dc21
                              2002015405

Acknowledgments

For Harriet, Eliza, and Nicholas

We would like to thank the following for permission to reproduce photographs: Corbis pp. 12 (Joe McDonald), 13 (Roger Tidman), 23 (O. Alamany & E. Vicens); Digital Stock p. 5; Digital Vision p. 21; FLPA pp. 14 (David Hosking), 15 (Minden Pictures/ Michael & Patricia Fogden), 20 (Minden Pictures/ Mitsuaki Iwago), 25 (Jurgen & Christine Sohns), 26 (Richard Dirscherl), 27 (Sunset); Natural History Museum p. 7; naturepl pp. 4 (Richard Du Toit), 6 (Hanne and Jens Eriksen), 18 (Francois Savigny), 19 (Dan Burton), 22 (Pete Oxford), 24 (Staffan Widstrand); Photolibrary pp. 9 (David B. Fleetham), 10 (David Courtenay), 11 (Geoff Higgins), 16 (OSF/Tim Shepherd), 17 (OSF/Paul Franklin), 29 (Tom Brakefield).

Cover photograph of a giraffe and an impala drinking at a waterhole, Botswana, reproduced with permission of FLPA/Frans Lanting.

We would like to thank Ann Fullick for her invaluable assistance in the preparation of this book, and Catherine Armstrong for her help with the first edition.

Every effort has been made to contact copyright holders of any material reproduced in this book. Any omissions will be rectified in subsequent printings if notice is given to the publisher.

Contents

Some words are shown in bold, **like this**. You can find out what they mean by looking in the glossary.

The natural world is full of an incredible variety of **organisms**. They range from tiny bacteria, too small to see, to giant redwood trees over 100 meters (330 feet) tall. With such a bewildering variety of life, it is hard to make sense of the living world. For this reason, scientists classify living things by sorting them into groups.

Classifying the living world

Sorting organisms into groups makes them easier to understand. Scientists try to classify living things in a way that tells you how closely one group is related to another. They look at everything about an organism, from its color and shape to the **genes** inside its **cells**. They even look at **fossils** to give them clues about how living things have changed over time. Then the scientists use all this information to sort the millions of different things into groups.

Scientists do not always agree about the group an organism belongs to, so they collect as much evidence as possible to find its closest relatives.

Mammals come in all shapes and sizes. Giraffes and antelopes are both mammals.

From kingdoms to species

Classification allows us to measure the **biodiversity** of the world. To begin the classification process, scientists divide living things into huge groups called **kingdoms**. For example, plants are in one kingdom, while animals are in another. There is some argument among scientists about how many kingdoms there are—at the moment most agree that there are five! Each kingdom is then divided into smaller groups called **phyla** (singular *phylum*), and the phyla are further divided into **classes**. The next subdivision is into **orders**. Within an order, organisms are grouped into **families** and then into a **genus** (plural *genera*), which contains a number of closely related **species**. A species is a single kind of organism, such as a mouse or a buttercup. Members of a species can reproduce and produce fertile offspring together.

Scientific names

Many living things have a common name, but these can cause confusion when the same organism has different names around the world. To avoid problems, scientists give every species a two-part Latin name, which is the same all over the world. The first part of the scientific name tells you the genus the organism belongs to. The second part tells you the exact species. Leopards, for example, have the scientific name *Panthera pardus*, while a lion is *Panthera leo*.

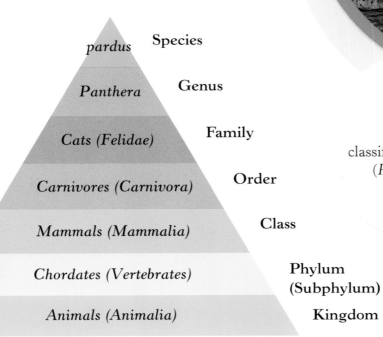

This diagram shows the full classification for a leopard (*Panthera pardus*).

pardus	Species
Panthera	Genus
Cats (Felidae)	Family
Carnivores (Carnivora)	Order
Mammals (Mammalia)	Class
Chordates (Vertebrates)	Phylum (Subphylum)
Animals (Animalia)	Kingdom

Within the animal **kingdom**, mammals are part of a group called the vertebrates. If you feel down the middle of your back, you can feel the bones of your spine (backbone). These bones are called vertebrae. Vertebrates are animals with backbones. Fish, amphibians, reptiles, birds, and mammals are all vertebrates.

What is a mammal?

Mammals have features in common that separate them from the other groups of vertebrates. Birds have feathers and reptiles are scaly, but mammals are usually hairy or furry. A few, such as dolphins and whales, have very little hair, but all mammals have hair somewhere!

Mammals are **endotherms**. This means their bodies stay at one temperature, no matter the temperature around them, because they make their own heat.

Fish, birds, reptiles, and amphibians all lay eggs, but most mammals give birth to live babies. All mammal mothers feed their young with milk made in their **mammary glands**. This is why they are called mammals.

Mammal milk is full of **nutrients**. Mammal babies like this camel grow quickly on this rich food.

The first mammals

Around 248 million years ago, before even the first dinosaurs appeared, a great **extinction** took place across Earth. More than 90 percent of all animal **species** died out. Many new types of animals appeared after this extinction. These included dinosaurs and the earliest mammals.

The early mammals were small insect-eaters like today's shrews. For millions of years they remained small, while the dinosaurs became the most successful large animals.

Then, about 65 million years ago, another great extinction wiped out the dinosaurs. But mammals survived, and many new species appeared because there was no longer competition from the dinosaurs for food and space.

Early mammals probably looked like this Morganucodon. This is a reconstruction of a mammal that lived during the Jurassic period.

Did you know ... where mammals come from?

Over thousands or millions of years, groups of living things may evolve (change) so that they are better **adapted** to their habitat (the place they live). This happens because living things that are better adapted live longer and produce more offspring. All the mammals we see today have evolved from a single group of **ancestors**.

There are about 4,600 **species** of mammals. They are grouped into 21 different **orders**.

The orders are shown in the table below.

Order	No. of species	Examples
Egg-laying mammals		
Monotremata (monotremes)	3	platypuses, echidnas
Pouched animals		
Marsupialia (marsupials)	272	kangaroos, wombats, koalas, opossums
Placental mammals		
Rodentia (rodents)	over 2,000	mice, rats, squirrels, voles, hamsters, beavers, porcupines
Chiroptera	925	bats
Insectivora (Insectivores)	375	shrews, moles, hedgehogs
Carnivora (Carnivores)	235	cats, dogs, wolves, foxes, badgers, weasels, stoats, mongooses, otters
Primates	233	lemurs, monkeys, apes, humans
Artiodactyla (artiodactyls)	220	sheep, cattle, pigs, goats, deer, antelopes, giraffes
Lagomorpha	80	rabbits, hares
Cetacea	79	whales, dolphins, porpoises
Pinnipedia	35	seals, walruses, sea lions
Xenarthra (edentates)	29	anteaters, armadillos, sloths
Dermoptera	2	colugos (flying lemurs)
Macroscelidea	19	elephant shrews
Scandentia	19	tree shrews
Perissodactyla	18	horses, zebras, donkeys, rhinos, tapirs
Pholidota	7	pangolins
Hyracoidea	7	hyraxes
Sirenia	4	manatees, dugongs
Proboscidea	2	elephants
Tubulidentata	1	aardvark

Sometimes it is hard to see why a group of species all belong to the same order. Weasels and polar bears, for example, do not look very similar, but they are both members of the same order (Carnivores). They are linked by the long teeth in their upper and lower jaws, which work together like a pair of scissors to slice through flesh.

Eggs and pouches

Most mammals give birth to live young. While the babies grow inside their mothers, they get food from a special **organ** called the placenta. They are called **placental mammals**.

However, in two mammal orders, the monotremes and the **marsupials**, things are different. Monotremes are very unusual mammals that lay eggs. There are only three monotreme species: two types of echidna and the duck-billed platypus. They are found in Australia and New Guinea. Monotremes count as mammals because they are furry and are **endotherms**, and because baby platypuses and echidnas feed on milk from their mother's **mammary glands**.

Marsupials, such as kangaroos and koalas, give birth to live young, but the newborn babies are extremely tiny and helpless. They spend their first weeks of life in the safety of their mother's pouch.

The duck-billed platypus—a unique mammal

- Furry body
- Endothermic
- Webbed feet
- Lays eggs
- Produces milk to suckle the young

Marsupials are named after the pouch (marsupium) that they carry their babies around in. They have this pouch because the young are helpless when they are born and need to be protected from **predators**. Koalas, kangaroos, wombats, bandicoots, opossums, and the Tasmanian devil are all familiar marsupials. Most marsupials live in Australia, but there are also marsupials in South America and one **species** in North America.

Plugging in to mom

Marsupial babies are born no bigger than honeybees. The only part that is well developed is one front claw. They use this claw to drag themselves from the birth canal to their mother's pouch. There, each baby fastens itself onto a teat and begins to drink milk. The teat swells in the baby's mouth, so the baby is firmly "plugged in" to its mother.

Baby marsupials suckle and stay in the pouch until they have grown enough to emerge—around 190 days for the red kangaroo! At first they leave the pouch only for a short time, but gradually they become completely independent.

Red kangaroo—the largest marsupial
- Furry body
- **Endothermic**
- Gives birth to live young
- Pouch in which young develop
- Produces milk

Tasmanian devils are fierce, carnivorous marsupials that may soon be extinct.

Bigfoot bounders

Kangaroos and wallabies are a **family** of marsupials that all have powerful back legs, large feet, and a long, muscular tail. Most of them graze on grass and are active at night. Because of their huge feet, the family is called the Macropodidae, which means "big feet."

When it is grazing, a kangaroo moves around on all fours, but when it senses danger it bounds away on its powerful back legs. A kangaroo's leap can take it 3 meters (10 feet) high and 10 meters (33 feet) along. It could clear a couple of cars in one jump.

Tasmanian devils

Tasmanian devils are rare marsupials found only in Tasmania. Sadly, the species is in danger of **extinction** in the wild within 20 years. It is infected with a terrible disease that causes face cancers and death. More than 80 percent of the animals in some areas are infected, and the disease is spreading rapidly. Scientists are taking healthy devils to mainland Australia, where they are **breeding** well. It may be possible to return them to Tasmania in years to come.

Chisel-Toothed Chewers

Mice, rats, voles, hamsters, squirrels, beavers, and porcupines are all rodents. Rodents are the biggest mammal **order**, with over 2,000 different **species**.

All rodents have long, strong front teeth called incisors, which they use for gnawing (chewing). The front of each incisor has a thin, very hard coating, while the back part of the tooth is a little softer. As a rodent gnaws at its food, the back of the tooth wears away more quickly, leaving the tooth with a razor-sharp edge. Most rodents use their incisors to eat nuts, seeds, leaves, and other plant food.

Fast breeders

Small rodents often have short lives, but many make up for this by producing large numbers of babies very quickly. Hamster mothers have up to 12 babies at once, and a lemming mother can produce more than 100 babies in 6 months! The babies are tiny, blind, and helpless when they are born, but they grow very quickly. A few rodents, such as beavers and the South American cavies, take longer to produce their young.

Flying squirrels have flaps of skin between their front and back legs, which they spread out into "wings" as they leap from tree to tree. They can glide long distances this way.

Rodent lifestyles

To avoid **predators**, many rodents rest during the day and feed at night. Many burrow into the ground, making holes and tunnels where they can rest in relative safety. Some, like the blind mole rats, spend their whole lives underground. Lemmings live in cold climates, and in the winter they dig tunnels under the snow instead of tunneling into the ground.

Some burrowers live alone, but others live in colonies (groups). Hundreds of prairie dogs, for instance, live together in enormous underground "towns."

Some rodents are tree-dwellers. Many squirrel species live in trees, but there are also tree rats, tree mice, and even tree porcupines.

Beavers, water rats, water voles, and coypus are all water-living rodents. Beavers and coypus eat only plants, but fish-eating rats are fierce water predators. Beavers are famous for blocking rivers or streams with dams to make lakes, where they build their homes.

Coypus originally come from South America, but people have introduced them to the United States and Europe, where they have survived and spread.

Do you know ... why rabbits aren't rodents?

Rabbits and hares have large incisor teeth, like rodents. But they also have a second pair of smaller incisors. This and other differences mean that rabbits and hares are not rodents, but are near relatives. They are classified in their own order, the lagomorphs.

Although birds may rule the air by day, at night bats are masters of the skies. Other mammals such as "flying" squirrels are good gliders, but bats are the only mammals that have wings and can fly. Unlike birds, which have wings made of feathers, a bat's wings are flaps of skin. The finger bones of the bat's "hands" have become enormously long to support this skin. The name for the bat **order** is Chiroptera, which means "hand wing."

Bats can be divided into two groups: the microbats and the megabats.

Megabats

Megabats are relatively large bats that eat fruit. They are also known as fruit bats. They have a good sense of smell as well as supersensitive night sight, and they use their noses to smell out the ripest fruit. Fruit bats live in warm, tropical countries where there is plenty of fruit for them to eat all year round.

Almost all bats roost upside down, hanging from a branch, the wall of a cave, or in a hollow tree trunk. In colder countries bats hibernate (sleep through the winter) in this way.

Microbats

Microbats are also known as insect-eating bats, because nearly all of them feed on insects. They also often live in groups. When female bats are having babies, they gather in colonies of up to 20 million. These colonies usually gather in caves.

Microbats have small eyes, because sight is not an important sense for them. They use sound to find their way around in the dark and to catch flying insects. As they fly, the bats send out a string of short, high squeaks. The squeaks are so high that people cannot hear them. These sounds echo off objects around the bat, and its sensitive ears pick up the returning echoes. The bats can use the echoes to build up an "echo picture" of the world around them. This is called **echolocation**.

Did you know ... vampire bats don't suck blood?

Vampire bats are tiny — the bat's body is only the size of a human thumb — and they feed on the blood of animals like cattle and horses. The bats find their **prey** by echolocation and make tiny cuts in the skin of an animal with their very sharp teeth. Chemicals in their saliva stop the blood from clotting, and they lap up blood as it flows. The animal doesn't even wake up, and there is no sucking involved!

An insectivore is an animal that eats mostly insects. Many mammals are insectivores, but there is also an **order** of mammals called the Insectivores. Shrews, moles, and hedgehogs are all Insectivores. They eat insects, spiders, worms, and other minibeasts.

Anteaters and armadillos are also insect-eaters. They belong to an order called edentates, which means "toothless."

Insectivores

Insectivores are small animals with long, sensitive noses. Most are **nocturnal** (active at night) and live on the ground or in burrows. They rely more on smell and touch than on their small eyes. Some insectivores are thought to be similar to the early **ancestors** of all **placental mammals**.

Three-fourths of Insectivores are shrews—mouse-like creatures with small ears and long noses. They eat insects and other small creatures. Shrews produce a strong smell that protects them from **predators**, and some **species** have a poisonous bite.

Moles have strong front legs and thick claws designed for digging. They dig deep burrows, with a central chamber and rings of tunnels around it. A mole's favorite food is worms, but it also eats insects and other animals.

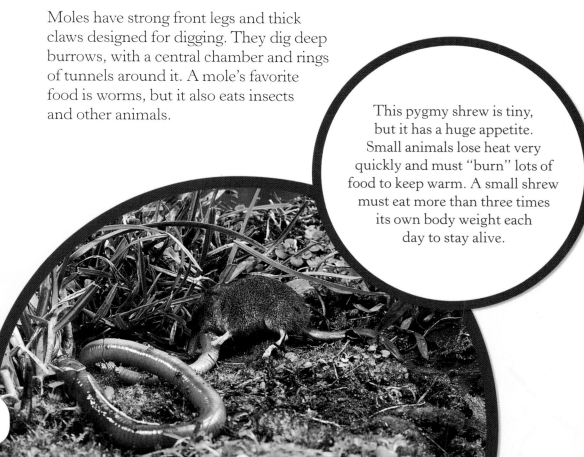

This pygmy shrew is tiny, but it has a huge appetite. Small animals lose heat very quickly and must "burn" lots of food to keep warm. A small shrew must eat more than three times its own body weight each day to stay alive.

Instead of fur, hedgehogs have a coat of sharp spines. When an enemy threatens them, they curl up into a prickly ball. In cooler climates, they hibernate (sleep through the winter).

Toothless mammals

The edentates are made up of insect-eating anteaters and armadillos, plus sloths, which are plant-eaters. The three groups look very different, but they are closely related. The bones of their lower backs are unique because they are fused together. Most live in South America. Anteaters have no teeth, but armadillos and sloths have small, simple, peg-like teeth. All have long, strong claws on their front feet.

Anteaters live on the ground or in trees. They eat only ants and termites, licking them up with a long, sticky tongue. Giant anteaters use their strong front claws to break open anthills and termite nests.

Armadillos have armor plating, which protects them from predators. In the daytime they sleep in burrows, and at night they roam around, using their claws to dig for insects. They can smell insects 20 centimeters (8 inches) below the surface.

Nine-banded armadillo— an edentate from the United States

- Eats insects
- Strong claws on front feet
- Peg-like teeth
- Armor plating
- Usually gives birth to four identical baby armadillos

Hoofed mammals are built for running. They have long legs and hard, horny hooves that protect their feet as they race along. Although they may not run as fast as some mammals, their hooves allow them to run for longer.

There are two different **orders** of hoofed mammals. Members of one group walk on two toes. These are the even-toed hoofed mammals, such as sheep, cattle, goats, pigs, antelopes, deer, camels, giraffes, and hippos. The other group is the odd-toed hoofed mammals. They walk on either three toes or one toe. Horses, zebras, rhinos, and tapirs are all odd-toed mammals.

Hoofed mammal lifestyles

Hoofed mammals are all herbivores (plant-eaters). Many live in open grassland or desert, where they need to be able to run fast to escape from big cats and other **predators**. Pigs, deer, goats, and llamas live in woodlands or mountain areas, where speed is less important.

Male hoofed mammals often have horns, tusks, or antlers, which they use as weapons and to impress females. Herds of hoofed mammals often **migrate** as the seasons change. Their babies can walk and run very soon after they are born.

Springboks do not just run from predators. They also scare them off by "pronking." Scientists think these huge jumps straight into the air signal to predators that the springbok is very fit and strong, and would be hard to catch.

Camels walk on two large, hoofed toes, which have tough, leathery pads underneath. When a camel puts its foot down, the toes spread. This is to stop it from sinking into the sand.

Tough food

Plant food, such as grasses and leaves, is difficult to **digest**. Hoofed animals need a special **digestive system** to break down this food. In odd-toed mammals, the intestines are very long— this is where most of the digestion happens.

Most even-toed animals are ruminants. This means that they have several stomachs and eat their food twice. They eat food quickly, and it goes into a big pouch called the rumen. Here, millions of microscopic **organisms** break down the tough **cell** walls that the animal cannot digest. The food then returns to the animal's mouth, and it chews again more slowly. This is called chewing the cud. After the ruminant swallows the food a second time, the food goes into another stomach, where normal digestion begins.

Do you know ... what the biggest land mammal ever was?

The biggest land mammal ever was a rhino-like hoofed animal called *Indricotherium*. It lived 25 to 30 million years ago in the regions of Pakistan, Mongolia, and China. It was twice as tall as an elephant and weighed more than 10 modern rhinos!

The word *carnivore* means "meat-eating animal." Many animals are carnivores, but there is also an **order** of mammals known as Carnivores. It includes cats, dogs, wolves, foxes, bears, badgers, and weasels. The feature that links all Carnivores is a pair of meat-slicing back teeth, called the carnassial teeth. Many Carnivores are meat-eaters, but some are omnivores (eat meat and plants), and one (the giant panda) is a vegetarian!

Catlike Carnivores

Cats, hyenas, mongooses, and civets are all related Carnivore **families**. All of them have retractable (can be drawn back in) claws. Hyenas have huge back teeth specialized for crunching bones, while mongooses are small, agile hunters that sometimes live together in colonies.

Many cats kill their **prey** with a bite to the back of the neck, using their canines (dagger-like teeth). However, big cats, such as lionesses, often kill large prey by clamping their jaws into the front of the animal's throat and suffocating it.

Cats are superb hunters. They have strong jaw muscles for a lethal bite, and their meat-slicing teeth are razor-sharp. They have excellent eyesight and good hearing.

Giant pandas look like bears but are more closely related to racoons. They are vegetarians, living almost entirely on bamboo shoots. Pandas are found only in a few places in China. They are among the world's most **endangered** animals.

Doglike Carnivores

Wolves, foxes, bears, racoons, and weasels are all doglike Carnivores. Unlike cats, they cannot retract their claws.

Wolves, wild dogs, and foxes are all part of the dog family itself. (The dogs we keep as pets are descended from wolves.) Like cats, they are hunters, but they also eat other food. Dogs rely on their sensitive noses to find prey. They do not lie in wait, but chase their prey instead. Wolves and wild dogs hunt in packs, while foxes hunt alone.

The racoon family and the bear family of Carnivores are closely related. Many of them are omnivores. Bears are the biggest of all carnivores. Kodiak and polar bears can weigh up to 1,000 kilograms (2,200 pounds), which is as much as a small car.

Weasels, stoats, badgers, and otters are known as mustelids. Most of this varied family are **predators**. Weasels and stoats have long, flexible bodies for chasing small animals along burrows or hunting them in the water. Badgers are worm specialists, while wolverines are fierce predators that can kill reindeer.

Lemurs, monkeys, apes, and humans are all primates. Most live in hot parts of the world, particularly in forests. Many primates are tree-dwellers, but a few **species**, such as baboons and humans, live on the ground. Primates have excellent eyesight and a good sense of touch. Their hands are designed for grasping things, and most have flat nails rather than claws.

Similar bodies, different behavior

Most primates have not become specialized for a particular lifestyle. Their hands and feet, for instance, are still similar to those of their early **ancestors**. Primates have **adapted** to the different places they live in by changing their behavior, rather than by changing their bodies. Although a human hand looks like that of a lemur, it is used for very different activities.

To learn new ways of behaving and to remember them, you need to have a big brain. Primates generally have large, complicated brains.

The majority of primates spend their lives in trees. Smaller monkeys and lemurs, like this Verreaux's sifaka, run along branches on all fours and leap from one tree to the next. Gibbons, other apes, and larger monkeys often swing from branch to branch instead.

Primate types

The biggest division within the primate **order** is between lemurs and their relatives and the monkeys and apes. Lemurs and related species such as bush babies have longer snouts than monkeys and apes, as well as wet noses like dogs. Their eyes are usually large, because most of them are night-feeders. Their ears are large and movable.

Monkeys have shorter faces than lemurs, dry noses, and smaller ears. Most South American (New World) monkeys can feel and hold onto things with their tails, whereas monkeys from Africa and Asia (Old World) cannot do this.

Apes include gibbons, orangutans, gorillas, chimpanzees, and humans. They do not have tails and have broad chests.

Growing and learning

Young primates have a lot to learn before they can survive by themselves. In addition to learning how to find food and avoid **predators**, they must learn how to fit in with their group. It takes two years for lemurs to become adults and ten years or more for gorillas, chimps, and humans.

Most primates have only one baby at a time. The baby clings onto its mother's fur from soon after birth and depends on her for food and care.

Some mammals have **adaptations** that allow them to live in water. The two biggest **orders** of sea mammals are the seals and walruses, and the whales and dolphins.

Flippered carnivores

Some scientists classify seals and walruses as Carnivores. Their **ancestors** are thought to have been similar to bears. They live in coastal seas, especially in cold polar areas, and their bodies have changed to suit their watery lifestyle.

Seals and walruses are **streamlined**, so they can move quickly through the water. Their ears are small or have disappeared, and they have a thick layer of blubber (fat) under their skin that keeps them warm. Their arms and legs have become broad, flat flippers. However, they need to breathe air and have their babies on land.

Like the Carnivores on land, seals and walruses eat meat. Seals eat fish, octopuses, crabs, and shrimp. Leopard seals and sea lions eat penguins. Walruses mostly eat shellfish from the seabed.

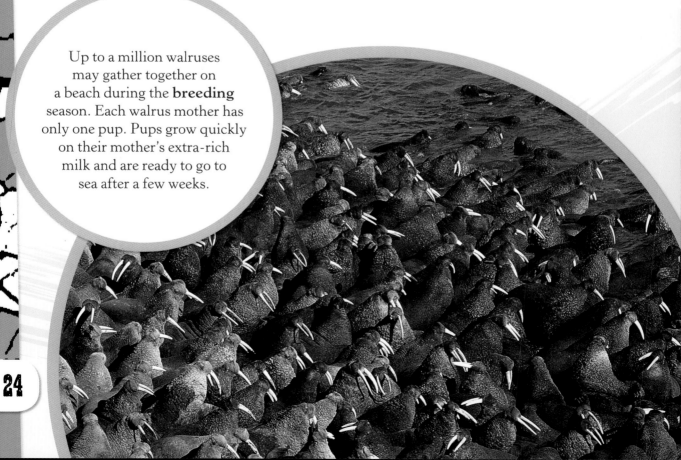

Up to a million walruses may gather together on a beach during the **breeding** season. Each walrus mother has only one pup. Pups grow quickly on their mother's extra-rich milk and are ready to go to sea after a few weeks.

Whales and dolphins

Whales and dolphins cannot survive on land. Their back limbs form a fishlike tail. In fact, they look more like fish than mammals, but they breathe air. They also give birth to live young and feed them on milk—all in the water!

Whales and dolphins can be divided into two groups: the baleen whales and the toothed whales. The largest whales, such as blue whales, fin whales, right whales, and humpback whales, are baleen whales. They are named after the sheets of horny material (baleen) that they have instead of teeth. To feed, the whales either swim through the water with their mouths open or take huge gulps of the ocean. The water escapes, but food (shrimp or small fish) is caught on the baleen and stays in the whale's mouth.

Toothed whales include dolphins, porpoises, killer whales, and sperm whales. They eat all kinds of sea creatures, from shrimp to seals. Killer whales sometimes eat other whales. Sperm whales feed on squid, which they catch from the ocean bottom. They can stay underwater for over two hours and dive to depths of up to 1,000 meters (3,300 feet).

Dolphin—intelligent whale

- Back limbs have become a tail
- Blowhole for breathing air
- Gives birth in water
- Lives in groups known as schools or pods
- Communicates using sound and movement
- Uses **echolocation** to find food

Do you know ... how big a blue whale is?

The blue whale is the largest animal that has ever lived. It can grow to 33 meters (110 feet) in length and weigh 150 tons.

We have seen that most mammals are hairy or furry, are **endothermic**, have four limbs (arms or legs), and feed their young on milk. But some mammals have become so completely specialized for the life they lead that they do not seem like mammals at all!

Fishy mammals

Dolphins and other toothed whales look similar to some fish, especially sharks. Like sharks, dolphins have **streamlined** bodies, fins, and a tail. Dolphins have up to 300 teeth, and sharks also have many teeth. Dolphins give birth to live babies, as do some types of shark. These similarities are mostly due to the fact that both sharks and dolphins are ocean **predators**. They need to be able to move quickly through the water to catch their **prey**.

Certain differences between sharks and dolphins, however, make it clear that they belong to separate **classes**. Like all fish, sharks have gills and can get the oxygen they need from water, whereas dolphins have lungs and must breathe air. Sharks cannot keep their bodies warm in cold water, whereas a dolphin's body temperature stays much the same no matter how warm or cold the water is. Shark babies also have to fend for themselves once they are born, whereas dolphin mothers feed their young on milk from their **mammary glands**.

The whale shark looks like a whale (a mammal). But it is a shark (a fish). The gill slits show that it gets oxygen from the water, not the air.

Flying mammals

Bats have some similarities to birds because both kinds of animal are **adapted** for flying. Both birds and bats have wings, and both are limited in how big they can grow, because they would become too heavy to fly. However, birds have feathers and beaks, whereas bats have furry bodies and a mouth with teeth. Also, birds lay eggs, while bats give birth to live young and feed them on milk.

Scaly mammals

Pangolins live in Africa and southern Asia. They have long noses and strong, clawed feet. The top of their bodies are covered in overlapping scales. They feed at night on ants and termites, which they dig out with their strong legs and lick up with a long tongue.

Because of their scales, you might think that pangolins are reptiles. But in fact they are mammals—they are endotherms, give birth to live young, and feed their babies on milk. Their scales are actually made from hairs.

Lost Forever?

The number of different types of living **organisms** in the world is often called **biodiversity**. Sadly, all over the world, **species** of living organisms are becoming **extinct**. This means that these organisms no longer exist on Earth. There are many different reasons for this. Extinction has always happened—some species die out and other species evolve (change). But today people are changing the world in ways that affect all other species.

People are destroying the places where animals live. We are cutting down rain forests and polluting the air and the water. Our use of fossil fuels, such as oil and gas, is causing global warming. Global warming is a rise in Earth's average temperature and a change in weather patterns. When the temperature and the weather change, it can have a serious effect on living things.

The circled areas are the ones where scientists think most mammal extinctions will happen in years to come.

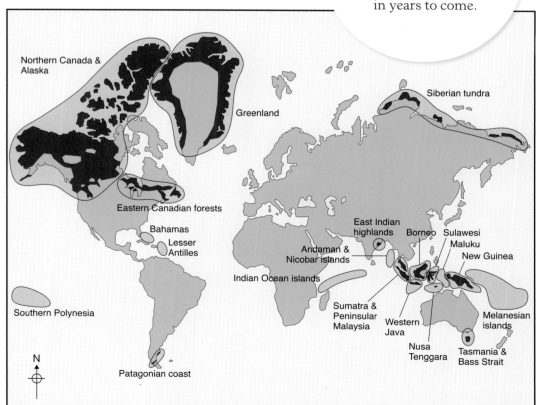

The United Nations fears that almost a quarter of all mammal species could be extinct within the next 30 years. That is over 1,000 types of mammals that you may never be able to show your grandchildren!

Some of the mammals that are threatened are well-known, for example, black rhinos, snow leopards, and Siberian tigers. Smaller mammals that are in danger, such as tenrecs, black-footed ferrets, and hyraxes, are less well-known. Scientists think that large mammals may be at more risk than smaller ones, because they often reproduce very slowly and there are fewer of them in the first place.

What can be done?

To help prevent mammals from becoming extinct, people need to take better care of Earth. If global warming can be stopped, many species will be saved. It is important to protect the places where mammals live. Biodiversity is important—we need as many species of mammals as possible for the future.

Snow leopard—beautiful but endangered

- Carnivore
- Member of the cat **family**
- Thick coat to protect it against cold
- Hunted for its coat
- 3,500 to 7,000 left in the wild

Glossary

adaptation gradual change of an organism over many years to fit into the place where it lives

ancestor relative from the past

biodiversity different types of organism around the world

breeding males and females producing young

cell smallest unit of life

class in classification, a large grouping of living things (for example, mammals), smaller than a phylum but bigger than an order

digest break down food in the body

digestive system part of an animal's body (the stomach, intestine, and bowel) that breaks down food so that it can be absorbed into the body

echolocation system that animals like bats use to "see" using sound. They make high-pitched sounds and build up a picture of their surroundings from the echoes that bounce back to them.

endangered in danger of becoming extinct (dying out altogether)

endotherm animal whose body temperature stays the same no matter the temperature around it

extinct when a species has died out and no longer exists

family in classification, a grouping of living things that is larger than a genus but smaller than an order

fossil remains of ancient living creatures found in rocks

gene structure by which all living things pass on characteristics to the next generation

genus (plural **genera**) in classification, a grouping of living things that is larger than a species but smaller than a family

kingdom in classification, the largest grouping of living things (for example, animals)

mammary glands milk-producing glands used to feed young on the belly or the chest of a female mammal

marsupial mammal whose young are born very tiny and undeveloped. Young marsupials live in a pouch on their mother's stomach.

migrate move between different parts of the world

nocturnal active at night

nutrient chemical from the digestion of food that nourishes our bodies

order in classification, a grouping of living things that is larger than a family but smaller than a class

organ part of the body that does a particular job

organism living thing

phylum (plural **phyla**) in classification, a grouping of living things that is bigger than an order but smaller than a kingdom

placental mammal mammal that gives birth to well-developed young

predator animal that hunts other animals for food

prey animal that is hunted by other animals for food

species group of living things that are all similar and can reproduce together

streamlined smooth body shape that allows mammals to move easily and quickly through water

Books

Animal Neighbors (series). New York: PowerKids, 2009.

Parker, Steve. *Eyewitness: Mammal.* New York: Dorling Kindersley, 2004.

Pyers, Greg. *Classifying Animals: Why Am I a Mammal?* Chicago: Raintree, 2006.

Snedden, Robert. *Living Things: Mammals.* Mankato, Minn.: Smart Apple Media, 2009.

Websites

www.historyforkids.org/scienceforkids/biology/animals/chordates/mammals/
This web page tells you all about mammals.

http://kids.yahoo.com/animals/mammals
On this web page there are lots of links to information about individual mammals.

www.mnh.si.edu
This is the website of the National Museum of Natural History in Washington, D.C.

http://nationalzoo.si.edu/Animals/SmallMammals/
This web page of the Smithsonian National Zoological Park in Washington, D.C., includes lots of interesting information about small mammals.

www.batcon.org
At this website you can find out more about bats.